Contents

Chapter 1

Hunger in the forest

Hansel and Gretel heard their stepmother shout, "Dinner!" and came running. It was only a slice of bread, but they were starving.

Their stepmother looked even more grumpy than usual. "What do you expect?" she snapped. "With so little money, all we can afford is bread."

The children's father sighed. "It's not my fault no one buys wood anymore," he said. "What with electric fires and plastic furniture..."

Oh, why did I marry a poor woodcutter?

Hansel and Gretel finished the last crumbs on their plates and went to their room.

"Poor Dad," yawned
Hansel. "Always in trouble."
He blew out the candle
and they tried to sleep.
Suddenly...

GROWL

"What's that noise?"
asked Gretel in a panic.

6

"Sorry," said Hansel. "It's my tummy. I was thinking of melted chocolate and toasted marshmallows."

"Oh don't!" Gretel begged. "I'm so hungry I can't sleep."

As they listened to their tummies rumble, they heard more nagging downstairs.

"The problem is," their stepmother was saying, "there's just not enough food for the four of us. The children will have to go."

"What?" cried the poor woodcutter.

How has it come to this?

"Do you have a better idea?" she sneered.

The woodcutter fell silent.
"Tomorrow, we'll take
Hansel and Gretel deep into
the forest," his wife continued,
"and leave them there!"

"But..." began the
woodcutter, sounding very sad.
"But what? You never know
– someone may find them and
take them home."

Chapter 2

Pebble path

That night, Gretel had nightmares about monsters in the woods. "I'm scared," she said, from under the covers. "What are we going to do?"

10

"Don't worry," said Hansel, who was lying wide awake. "I have an idea."

Quietly, he tiptoed outside. White pebbles gleamed in the moonlight. He collected as many as he could and stuffed them into his pockets.

"Wake up, my little sugar plums," called the stepmother, soon after dawn. "We're going on a lovely walk today!"

Hansel squeezed Gretel's hand as they left the house, pretending they knew nothing.

"Hurry up, Hansel!" said his stepmother after a while. She didn't see him drop pebbles, one by one, behind him.

The sad woodcutter walked on ahead, his head down and his shoulders hunched.

"Perhaps the children should rest," said the stepmother finally. They were standing in a gloomy clearing. "You two sit here, while your father and I... um... cut some wood."

"I'll make you a fire first," said the woodcutter.

"Come on!" called his wife impatiently. And she dragged her husband into the forest.

A ghostly mist hung over the clearing. Hansel warmed his hands by the fire. "Cheer up, Gretel," he said, trying to smile. They lay down on some squishy moss and were soon fast asleep.

Twit-twoo

What was that?

"Wake up!" cried Gretel, shaking Hansel. "It's already dark... and I'm freezing!"

16

"What... where..." said Hansel, looking around him. The mist had gone and a pebble gleamed in the moonlight. "Let's go," he said, taking Gretel's hand.

His pebble trail led them through the shadowy forest and all the way home.

Chapter 3

A trail of crumbs

"Hansel! Gretel!" called the woodcutter in surprise.

The stepmother heard their names and froze. "Drat," she snarled. "They're back."

"We're starving,"
moaned Hansel.

"Well, I didn't save
you any lunch – or dinner,"
said his stepmother.

"What about breakfast?"
Gretel asked.

"Here, you can have my
bread," said the woodcutter.

His wife scowled at him.

That evening, Hansel and
Gretel were relieved to be in
their own room. But they
didn't trust their stepmother
at all.

What's she
saying, Hansel?

With his ear to the door,
Hansel heard the stepmother's
voice grow louder.

20

"We'll take them deeper into the forest this time," she declared. "They'll never find their way out!"

"You heartless woman," muttered the woodcutter.

"What?" she barked. "Do you want us all to starve?"

Hansel and Gretel lay trembling in their beds. When all was quiet, Hansel crept off to find more pebbles. But he couldn't open the front door. His stepmother must have locked it.

What do I do now?

"Wakey-wakey, rise and shine," said the stepmother, early next morning.

22

She forced Hansel and Gretel
out of bed, gave them a slice
of stale bread to share and
marched them into the forest.

Hansel's tummy
was grumbling but he
didn't eat his half of the bread.
Instead, he crumbled it along
the way to leave a second trail.

Soon, the trees were so thick they blocked out the sky.

"Another lovely place for a rest," said their stepmother, cheerfully.

The woodcutter sighed and made a fire. He couldn't bear to look at his children.

"Don't panic," Hansel said
to Gretel, when they were
alone. "We can follow the
breadcrumbs home."

He turned to see a blackbird
pecking at a crumb. "Shoo!" he
cried, chasing the bird away.
A woodpecker swooped down
and took another crumb.
"No!" shouted Hansel.

Birds twittered from every tree. Hansel and Gretel looked for more crumbs, but not a single one was left.

"What do we do now?" asked Gretel, shivering.

I'll think of something.

Chapter 4

The hidden house

By morning, Hansel
still didn't have a plan.
"Let's just walk until
we find the edge of the
forest," suggested Gretel.

All day they walked, past tall trees and spiky branches. Night fell and still they stumbled on.

By the following morning, they were faint from hunger. The spooky forest seemed to go on forever.

At noon, they finally
staggered into a clearing.
There, in the distance, stood
a little house.

"Let's see if anyone's in,"
said Gretel. "They might
give us some food."

As the pair neared the house, a delicious smell wafted past.

"Freshly baked cakes!" cried Gretel. She ran closer... and gasped. The walls were made from chunks of cake and the roof was glistening chocolate.

Pink sponge bricks!

"It looks scrumptious," she said, hardly believing her eyes.

"And tastes even better," mumbled Hansel, already munching on a windowsill.

Even the windows smelled sweet. Gretel licked one. "It's sugar!"

And a gingerbread door!

Hansel was trying to bite off the toffee apple doorknocker, when the door flew open.

"Aaaargh!" he yelled, as an old woman hobbled out.

She was as wide as a barrel and uglier than a toad. Her bulging eyes fixed on the two children and she smiled, showing her rotten teeth.

"Enjoying my house, are you?" she croaked.

"Yes, it's delicious... I mean delightful," said Gretel, quickly wiping chocolate from her face.

"You must come inside," said the old woman.

I love visitors.

Chapter 5

Tricked!

Hansel and Gretel couldn't
believe their luck. In seconds,
the kind woman laid out a
magnificent meal for them.

"Would you like to stay the night?" she asked.

Hansel and Gretel could only nod. Their mouths were full of cookies and candy.

Our tummies won't keep us awake tonight!

Gretel woke up to see sun
streaming onto Hansel's bed.
But Hansel wasn't there. "I bet
he's already eating breakfast,"
she thought and ran to join him.

"You're just in time to help
me cook," croaked the old
woman, no longer smiling.

Gretel politely peeled potatoes, chopped carrots and grated cheese.

The ugly woman bossed Gretel around all morning, until she had prepared a feast.

"Now put it through the hatch in the shed outside," the woman ordered.

Gretel was confused. She went outside and heard her brother yelling from the shed.

"Hansel! What's happened?" called Gretel.

"That woman's a witch," he shouted. "She's trapped me with a spell. Now she wants to fatten me up... and eat me."

A cold shiver crept up Gretel's spine. "Don't worry," she said, sounding braver than she felt. "We'll trick her and escape."

Chapter 6

Into the oven

That evening, the witch hobbled over to Hansel's shed. "Hold out your finger," she shouted. "Show me how plump you are."

She reached into the hatch
and Hansel held up a twig.

"Dear me," sighed the
witch. "You're all bone.
Eat more, boy!"

For days, she made poor
Gretel cook enormous meals.
Hansel ate every mouthful,
but his twig finger never got
any fatter.

Hansel and Gretel's plan was working... but the witch was growing impatient.

"Plump or skinny, I'm eating your brother tomorrow," she announced one evening.

No!

Gretel lay awake all night. "I won't let that horrible witch near my brother," she thought.

"Gretel," the witch shouted at dawn. "Get inside the oven and check how warm it is."

"No," Gretel replied.

"What?" cried the witch.

"I... um... can't fit in there."

"Of course you can, you silly little brat."

No really. I think my head's too big.

By now, the witch was very annoyed. "My oven is *huge*," she said. "Look, even I can fit inside." And, with a puff and a pant, she clambered in.

Quick as a flash, Gretel slammed the oven doors shut.

As the wicked witch frazzled in her own oven, her spell on the shed was broken.

"Gretel!" called Hansel, running into the house. "You've saved me."

And I've cooked the witch!

Safe at last, Hansel and Gretel searched the witch's house for goodies. They took some jewels and a basket of snacks, then set off into the trees.

Taking pity on Hansel and Gretel, the birds showed them the way home.

The woodcutter was overjoyed to see them. As for their stepmother – she wasn't there.

She left me to live in a new brick house.

"Look, Dad," said Gretel, showing him the jewels. "You don't need to worry now. We can have a feast every night."

"And a new toffee doorknocker each day," added Hansel.

Hansel and Gretel was first written down by Jacob and Wilhelm Grimm. The brothers lived in Germany in the early 1800s and together they retold hundreds of fairy tales.

Series editor: Lesley Sims

Cover design by Russell Punter

First published in 2005 by Usborne Publishing Ltd., Usborne House, 83-85 Saffron Hill, London EC1N 8RT, England. www.usborne.com
Copyright © 2005 Usborne Publishing Ltd.